Southwest Writers Series **24**
General Editor: James W. Lee

Erna Fergusson

BY DAVID A. REMLEY

University of New Mexico

52900

STECK-VAUGHN COMPANY   AUSTIN, TEXAS

A Californian by birth, David A. Remley grew up in Indiana. He graduated from Wabash College in 1953, then attended Harvard University as a MacIntosh Fellow. He received his M.A.T. degree from Harvard in 1954, and his Ph.D. degree in American Literature and American History from Indiana University in 1967. Dr. Remley has taught in Indiana junior and senior high schools and at the University of Colorado. He is currently Assistant Professor of American Literature and American Studies at the University of New Mexico. His scholarly articles have appeared in the *Indiana Magazine of History* and the *Midcontinent American Studies Journal*. His free-lance articles have appeared in national newspapers and magazines.

The author acknowledges with gratitude the permission of Alfred A. Knopf to quote from their published works of Erna Fergusson.

Library of Congress Catalog Card Number 75-92553
Copyright © 1969 by Steck-Vaughn Company, Austin, Texas
All Rights Reserved. Printed and Bound in the United States of America

Erna Fergusson

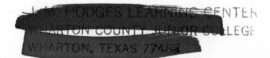

Erna Fergusson

H. L. MENCKEN's *American Mercury* carried an article by Erna
Fergusson in August, 1931. In the "Editorial Notes" Mencken
printed a biographical sketch she had sent him. It gave the
essential facts of her life to that date. She had been brought up
in Albuquerque, in the old town. Since girls were supposed to be
"ladies," she had been sent first to a private school, later to a boarding school, and from time to time to the public school. During
this period she had, she told Mencken, been making her own private observations of the town.

After a while she received a degree from the University of New
Mexico and still another from Columbia University. She turned,
then, to teaching school because it seemed to be expected of her.
When World War I started, Erna Fergusson became a Red
Cross worker and supervisor. As she wrote Mencken, "I ran around
all over the State fixing things up for Mexican soldiers who had en-
listed under a couple of names, for mothers who asked me what
the ocean was, and for wives who had forgotten to marry" ("Editorial Notes," p. xx).

When the war was over, she began to dude wrangle. She
led tourists all over Arizona, New Mexico, and southern Colorado
to see the Indian ceremonials. The tours often involved hardships.
"They blamed me bitterly for almost everything," she wrote
Mencken of the tourists, "but some of them liked it and came
again" ("Editorial Notes," p. xx). But Erna's venture was successful enough that the Santa Fe Railroad and Fred Harvey, deciding

1

to go into the tour business on a big scale, bought her company out and hired her to train their girl guides, whom they named "couriers." Erna was "Chief Courier" for the big venture—the Santa Fe's "Indian Detour."

What she failed to tell Mencken was that she was already a successful writer (her book *Dancing Gods* [1931] had stimulated a wide public interest in the Southwestern Indian dances), that she had gotten her start as a journalist on the old Albuquerque *Herald* and the *New Mexico Highway Journal*, that the Koshare Tours she conducted had given the impetus for *Dancing Gods*, and that her childhood in a territory only recently saved for "progress" from the Indians and Spanish Americans had provided the enduring interest from which all her writing would follow. While she traveled much, got a young American woman's literary education in private schools and in the universities, and knew Europeans and Easterners, the world which she loved and wrote about was the Southwest she had known as a child and as a tour guide in the back country of New Mexico. If she later broadened her reach to cover Mexico, Hawaii, and the Latin American countries, it was as an extension of interest into the cultural backgrounds of the world of her childhood. Her brothers, Harvey and Francis, had left the home country—Harvey to transpose it into fiction and a delightful autobiography, Francis to be a drama critic and professor at Rutgers. But Erna chose to remain, to live in and write about her country in firsthand accounts. Like Thoreau, Erna was to travel much in Concord. Unlike Thoreau, she was not essentially a social critic. Yet her books are often critical, by implication if not directly. The body of her work gives a balanced view of both the pleasant and unpleasant aspects of a geographical region and a varied culture. If she ever felt herself a rebel, it does not show in her writing. The final product is an affirmative description of a heritage she felt positively about.

Her persistent optimism and intellectual clarity seem also to date

2

from childhood. She was the oldest of four children of a New Mexican family which had participated fully in the American dream of success. Her father, Harvey Butler Fergusson, had come to the Territory in 1881 as a young lawyer checking a mining claim for an Eastern client. In the roaring town of White Oaks, he raised a cabin with three other promising young men: Emerson Hough, Albert Bacon Fall, and William MacDonald (later governor of New Mexico). White Oaks in those days was a place where everyone was going about building a fortune or confidently expecting to build one. Harvey Butler Fergusson hung out his shingle, took in clients, and immediately caught the gold fever. "I think his early years in White Oaks were among the happiest of his life," his son Harvey Fergusson, Jr. wrote. "He . . . rattled about the country in a buckboard, peering into holes that might contain millions, studying ores with a microscope. He foregathered with other young men in bars and on street corners to talk the fascinating lore of drift and ledge and vein and assay. He even bought a six-shooter and carried it in a pocket holster" (*Home in the West: An Inquiry into My Origins*, p. 64).

Harvey Butler Fergusson's experience in White Oaks must have been a happy new beginning for a man who had had until this time a depressing life. His father, Sampson Noland Ferguson (the family later changed the spelling to *Fergusson*, with a double s), had lost his fortune in land and slaves in Alabama with the defeat of the Confederacy. Harvey Butler Fergusson, raised in the antebellum South of horses, hunting, slaves, fish fries, and month-long family visits, was thirteen years old when the War began. At its end, he was, like thousands of ex-Confederates after the War, out on his own. Pushed by his family, he enrolled at Washington College in Virginia with nearly all his father had left to give a promising son: a personal letter to the new president, General Robert E. Lee.

Seven years later, Harvey Butler Fergusson left the college. He

3

had worked his way through by doing odd jobs, by pitching hay in summer, and by teaching school in the mountains in the winter. He came to think of himself as romantically defiant, unable to accept defeat. He told his own son much later that on winter mornings in his bare room at the college he had to smash the ice in the water pitcher in order to wash his face. "That ice-smashing act seemed to stand in his memory as the supreme symbol of his hardships and his defiance of them. His repeated descriptions of it made a deep impression upon me," Harvey Fergusson, Jr. wrote (*Home in the West*, p. 62). Erna must have heard the same descriptions. Beside them, her father's talk of his new life in White Oaks sounded like arrival in Heaven. Young man gone West had made good! Erna's positive attachment to New Mexico no doubt started in the hope and the sense of success the Territory had given her father.

Harvey Butler Fergusson was also a skeptic of the frontier sort. Although he was sentimental about his past and romanticized the bad years in Alabama and Virginia into personal triumphs for inflexible self-discipline and hard work, he renounced unequivocally the religion his mother had wrestled to teach him and firmly believed Darwin's theories were clear-cut fact. It was a day when general opinion held that a man could believe either in Darwin or in God, but not both. Harvey Fergusson, Jr. recalls that his father explained evolution and asserted that all men were directly descended from the apes. As proof, he claimed that some men have vestigial tails existing as an extra vertebra at the bottom of their spines. "We were brought up without religious training," wrote Erna's sister, "and none of the family ever went to church. As children we were sometimes taken to Sunday School by our little friends . . . but with no visible effect" (letter from Lina F. Browne to David A. Remley, September 28, 1968). Erna herself never joined any church, and her criticism of the narrow-mindedness of

4

frontier Protestants and the aggressiveness with which their missionaries upset the Indian cultures probably started with her father's critical skepticism and his bravely standing outside the church door.

Like her father, Erna was a lifelong Democrat; unlike him, however, she was not active in politics. Harvey Butler Fergusson first became a successful Albuquerque lawyer and then a renowned party orator and office seeker. He never refused to stump for a fellow partisan in trouble with the voters, and he had the essential ability to weld a coalition of strange bedfellows—Spanish Americans mad at the Republican machine and nesters rolling west to New Mexico out of Texas. He was elected delegate from the Territory and later was twice elected U.S. Representative from the State of New Mexico. Harvey Fergusson, Jr. remembers that he had a lifelong sympathy with the poor in their struggle against rich oppressors, with the humble against the distant villains of Wall Street. "I well remember," Harvey Fergusson, Jr. wrote, "that on hunting trips in the back country I could seldom ride into one of the little adobe towns, with its herds of goats and its patches of chile, without meeting a Mexican who would give me anything I wanted because I was my father's son. 'I am a Republican but I vote for your father because he is my friend'" (Home in the West, p. 72). Certainly Erna inherited her passionate interest in New Mexico's oppressed people from her father. Her most vigorous writing about the Southwest occurs in her descriptions of the threatened cultures of the Spanish American and the Indian.

The other powerful figure in the lives of the Fergusson children was Grandfather Franz Huning, who lived in "Huning Castle" in Old Town Albuquerque while the young Fergussons were growing up. Important, self-made, moderately wealthy, philosophical, somewhat eccentric, Huning had arrived in the Territory on Christmas day of 1849, a German immigrant and a bullwhacker

5

on the Santa Fe Trail. He quickly made friends with the native New Mexicans, lived among them, and learned their language. In less than a year he was speaking, reading, and writing Spanish.

Using Franz Huning's memoirs, his grandson Harvey has sketched a young adventurer fascinated by the local people—he was intimate with both bandit and priest—who also had an intellectual passion for fact and logic. Huning apparently wished to root out some of the superstitions of his New Mexican friends, and he hotly debated their acceptance of the power of the local faith healers. He even protested a prayer for rain one day, opposing the event until he and the supplicants were gullywashed by a prairie thundershower. "Thrown on the defensive but undaunted," his grandson wrote, "he pointed out that many another prayer had not brought a drop of rain, whereupon his friends replied simply, 'God knows best' " (Home in the West, p. 27).

During the early years in the Territory, Franz Huning went on a trading expedition to the Apaches in the Gila River country. He kept a diary, started a dictionary of the Apache language, and collected various items of Apache culture. After a financially unsuccessful trip, he returned to Santa Fe, then moved to Albuquerque, where he took a job as a clerk in a store. He soon dropped that to become secretary to the vicar of the Catholic diocese and, later, secretary and interpreter to the local federal judge. In 1857 he opened his own small store on the plaza. From that time on, he was a successful merchant and trader, making many trips to St. Louis for wagon loads of dry goods. He built a flour mill, a sawmill, and a small empire in land and cattle. Later he built the square-towered home in Old Town called Huning Castle, surrounded by grape arbors, cottonwood groves, orchards, pastures, sloughs, and a duckpond with an island and an arched wooden bridge.

Erna and her brothers and sisters knew their grandfather as the aged master of Huning Castle. "My grandfather doubtless thought

6

of this place as the crown of his success," Harvey Fergusson, Jr. wrote, "but as he aged it became more and more his refuge from a society he neither liked nor understood" (*Home in the West*, p. 44). As an old man, Franz walked to the mill every day, went home to Huning Castle to water his gardens, then turned in late afternoon and evening "to the long readings in several languages which had occupied his youth and to the long thoughts of a solitary and reflective man" (*Home in the West*, p. 44). He liked neither the land-grabbing railroaders and the "new town" they built, nor the kings of business and politics who came in with the end of the century. He had always been morally stern, accustomed to dealing by mutual understanding, and intolerant of the weaknesses and stupidities of his fellows. His own moral prejudices put him badly out of date in a corrupt world. As he aged he became more distant from all but his closest friends.

His grandchildren apparently knew him but slightly while he lived, though no doubt they saw him nearly every day. Erna mentions that he told them stories. Their home, Glorietta (now the Manzano Day School at 1801 Central, N.W.), was just across the street from Huning Castle. Harvey Fergusson, Jr. wrote that his grandfather's estate was his second home. Apparently, the old man had little interest in converting the grandchildren. "He talked to me a little but never about himself or his adventures and he never gave me anything like a lecture," Harvey Fergusson, Jr. wrote (*Home in the West*, p. 47).

Erna's writings seldom mention her family. She maintains a dignity and silence about them, but there is little doubt that many of her own traits and tastes are inherited from the childhood contact with her grandfather and with the family stories about him. Her fundamental distaste for the new society the railroad brought in and her love of the old Southwesterner of the pre-railroad days appear in Erna's writing, though perhaps unconsciously; she thought of herself as a modern woman, not given to worshipping the past and trying to prevent the future. Nevertheless, the condescension and the love are there, and they are of the very spirit of her grandfather. "Such a country," she writes, "inscrutable, unconquerable, and like nothing his kind had ever seen before, naturally affected the man who dared to face it. It made, in fact, a new type of man who may renew himself in other challenging conditions or who may prove to be only a passing phase due to submerge in the babbitry which has come in with trains" (*Our Southwest*, p. 14).

Like her grandfather, she was absorbed in the country and the people of the Southwest. Her most popular book, *Dancing Gods*, reveals that penchant for observation and description suggested by her grandfather's study of the Spanish and Apache languages and his keeping of journals. Also like her grandfather, she was a student, a reader. Most of her writing expresses an understanding of other cultures and suggests how the Anglo-American might interact with them for the richer preservation of the best in all. The fact that she made a living as a tour guide and a travel writer put her in an excellent position to serve as lackey to the chambers of commerce. But just as her grandfather would have done, she tried to present a clear picture of the realities of life in the Southwest and in Latin America. She never described that life as easy or the country as rich in resources panting for exploitation. Like her grandfather, Erna in her best work was "instinctively a scientist and writer first, a merchant incidentally if at all" (*Home in the West*, p. 29).

Erna was clearly a brave child. Harvey Fergusson, Jr. recalls his sister's presence at a dinner for William Jennings Bryan. Bryan had been reading Tolstoy. Between cavernous mouthfuls of chicken and dressing, the great man spoke upon Christian conversion. "My sister Erna," Harvey Fergusson, Jr. wrote, "had read

Tolstoy too, and was the only other present who had. She chirped bravely back at the great man while my father beamed with delight and I sat silent, filled with envy but definitely not giving a damn whether Tolstoy had rediscovered the true Jesus or not" (*Home in the West*, p. 106). She could also be the domineering older sister. Harvey Fergusson, Jr. wrote of her that he "always regarded her as something of a nuisance and occasionally as an active enemy because she had a tendency to tease and ridicule me. The little girls she brought to the house were no better" (*Home in the West*, p. 176).

Erna received an A.B. from the University of New Mexico in 1912. A year later she took the M.A. in history at Columbia. The degrees had followed several years of travel. She had been in Washington with her father, then a U. S. Congressman from New Mexico, she had visited her grandmother in Europe, and she had been to the Girls' Collegiate School in Los Angeles. For a short time after receiving the degree from Columbia, she taught school, first at Chatham Hall in Virginia, then in the Albuquerque Public Schools.

With the coming of World War I she took the job of Red Cross Home Service Secretary and State Supervisor for New Mexico. Now she had the chance she had really been waiting for without quite knowing it—to travel into the back country and the small towns of her home state to get acquainted with the people. Erna's life's work as a popular cultural historian and commentator on the Southwest got its start in this period almost by accident. After the War, she would create ways of making a living from her firsthand knowledge of the country she loved best.

Her friend Dorothy Woodward says that Erna told her (no doubt with tongue in cheek) that her life "followed a very logical pattern," and that "one thing leads naturally to another" ("Erna Fergusson," p. 75). Clearly, in the period after World War I, one

9

thing was leading to another for Erna Fergusson. Having discovered that she wanted to travel more in New Mexico, Erna thought of attempting a pioneering venture with another New Mexican woman, Ethel Hickey. Could they turn their traveling and their broad experience of the Southwest into a self-supporting venture? In 1921, Erna and Ethel Hickey decided to try.

They founded a tour company, the "Koshare Tours," and sent out colorful brochures with representations of Southwestern Indian scenes. The brochures described several regular tours and were headlined "Seeing the Southwest: The Koshare Way." Not only did the guests get Erna's personal guide services, but their comforts were carefully planned as well. For tours of more than a day, elaborate campouts were arranged so that when the touring cars came lugging in, the guests found tents and cots set up and waiting. Professional cooks prepared the meals, and the drivers of the open-topped touring cars were indefatigable with spade, jack, and wrench. Her files for the period are filled with letters of appreciation from ex-guests everywhere. Some, returning home, wrote humorous poems about the tour, expressing a good natured attitude toward the discomforts of car and camp. The evidence is clear that Erna's planning and presence had made the tour memorable.

At about the time she founded the Koshare Tours, Erna began writing local color articles for the Albuquerque *Herald*. In 1922-23 a series of these appeared under the title "Do You Remember?" Although sometimes dull and stylistically awkward, the articles contain amusing descriptions of the old Albuquerque Erna had known as a child around the turn of the century. "Do You Remember?" is important for Erna as a writer, not only because it is her first extended venture into print, but also because it shows her practicing two techniques she mastered later in her books—the interview and the informal, almost conversational prose style. With such titles as "Freighting Across the Plains," "The First Train," and "The

First Street Car," the articles are anecdotes gathered from interviews of Albuquerque's old-timers and written in a relaxed manner.

"Do You Remember?" also reveals an attempt at that characteristic technique of American humor, exaggeration. Erna experiments with it somewhat successfully in these sketches of the past; but she could not adapt it to her later studies of Indian and Spanish culture, and it appears hardly at all elsewhere in her writing.

Her next important event as a writer was the sale of two articles to Century Magazine in 1926. Having learned from her experience with the Herald that she could interest a local audience on hometown subjects, she now strove to reach a national audience interested in the Southwest.

Of the two articles in Century Magazine, the first, "From Redskins to Railroads," is the most original. A concise description of Spanish Colonial life in New Mexico, the article is an excellent portrait of the lives of both ricos and pobres. The last few paragraphs suggest the same displeasure with the railroads which Erna's grandfather had felt so strongly, that nostalgia for the old Southwest that Erna never quite shook off: "Broken bits are left here and there—stately courtesy in the remote villages, remnants of old morality plays, soft-toned Spanish speech—but these too will soon pass. What happened to it all? The blast of a steam-whistle . . . . Progress went on . . . with the inexorable rudeness of progress, and in 1880 the first train steamed into Albuquerque" ("From Redskins to Railroads," pp. 30-31).

The second article, "From Rodeo to Rotary," contains much of the material which had appeared in "Do You Remember?" Erna often used material which had appeared in her earlier articles, though usually in carefully revised form. While the style is much improved, the condensation of "From Rodeo to Rotary" takes the pleasure out of the reading. The account of Albuquerque's first streetcar, for instance, is much more concise but far less entertaining than the earlier telling. The sense of leisure is no more. Phrasings have undergone interesting changes, suggesting that Erna was professionalizing her style for a wider audience.

Her third important article, "New Mexico's Mexicans," appeared in 1928. It belongs in the same series as the two previous *Century* articles because its subject is the old culture of New Mexico and the problems of coming into the gringo twentieth century. Erna shows how the leisurely style of the native New Mexican, the close-knit family life, and the authoritarian tradition in law and politics conflict with the Anglo-American emphasis on hard work, personal development, and independence of view: "The Mexican frankly hates work and refuses to be bullied into believing that he loves it .... he admires authority and is quite willing to be bullied into anything not work" (p. 438). She uses here an amusing story to illustrate the old-fashioned native's absolute loyalty to the Hidalgo's political views. The sixteen voters of a precinct, all sheepmen, came down from the hills to vote on election day. Not having heard from the don, a Republican, they asked the railroad ticket agent which man to vote for. Having a sense of humor, he advised the Democrat, whereupon sixteen votes were cast for that candidate and the ballot box was locked up. Then a messenger arrived from the don instructing the sixteen to vote for the other candidate, the Republican. Undaunted, the sheepmen insisted that the box be reopened and their ballots changed.

Erna's understanding of the conflict of civilizations in the Southwest is apparent throughout the article. "Neither the background nor the training ·of most of the pioneers," she writes, "qualified them to appreciate a fine old civilization. Many of them came from the Southern States, where a dark skin could have only one meaning. The result was they assumed that Mexicans, being different, were inferior" ("New Mexico's Mexicans," p. 440). She recognizes also the importance of the immediate demands of life on

12

the frontier: "A man who is one jump ahead of a savage doesn't meditate on the graces of a foreign people. He does what he can to stabilize life for himself and his family .... The result in New Mexico was that the Americans acquired the country ..." (p. 441).

Erna's empathy with the native New Mexican is most interesting. She had developed her sensibility from direct contact with the natives during her stints as a Red Cross worker and a tour guide: "During the war charming incidents came to light of how Mexicans made their Red Cross and governmental visitors feel at home. They attentively listened to lectures on matters they had known for generations .... Whatever the visitor says is right .... the stranger thinks he is gathering information, when all he gets is a polite reflection of what he says" (p. 441).

In a short story, "Justice as Interpreted," Erna contrasts, but oversimplifies, Anglo and Spanish concepts of freedom and justice in the Southwest. There has been a vast amount of argument over how much and what kind of freedom the individual experienced on the Spanish and Mexican frontier. Salvador de Madariaga states the opposite poles of the argument succinctly in his great *Rise of the Spanish American Empire* (New York: The Free Press, 1965). He attacks the widely held concept that Spanish American communities have historically suffered, and continue to suffer, from the lack of an initial training in the "art of self-government." How else, he asks, could countries as far removed from Spain as were the Indies have been governed, if not, in fact, by themselves? He also suggests that those who cling to this concept in their writings make the mistake of holding up—either explicitly or by implication—the contrasting example of England's "superior political wisdom," as if, from the very beginning, England had established parliamentary institutions in her own colonies and unselfishly looked forward to the day when these colonies could govern themselves!

Madariaga's point is that there was actually a great deal of free-

13

dom on the Spanish frontier, both in commercial exploits and the creation of imaginative means of handling local problems of justice. This is the point of Erna Fergusson's short story "Justice as Interpreted." Boleslo Aragon, a young New Mexican without education or wealth, uses his natural talents—muscularity, great shrewdness, and a widely recognized handiness with the gun—to advance his own interests on the frontier. He applies for a job as "interpreter" and, by unspoken understanding, as bodyguard to one Judge Meeks, recently appointed to the federal court at Roswell and recently arrived from Kansas. Unequipped for the frontier with anything but his Eastern, abstract standards of justice, and, therefore, terrified by actual frontier conditions, Judge Meeks instantly feels the need of a reliable sidekick thoroughly trained in the rough arts of this dangerous place. Recognizing his "usefulness," seeing the opportunity to "make the best" of his special talents, Boleslo hires himself out to Judge Meeks. When offered seven dollars a day to act as interpreter, "with elaborate Spanish courtesy, he expressed his regrets." Whereupon, the Judge offers an additional three dollars a day. "And my expenses," Boleslo adds, closing the deal (p. 3).

What then develops is a power struggle between Boleslo (who is much the shrewder) on the one hand and an abstract, Anglo concept of justice (represented by Judge Meeks and the Roswell district attorney) on the other. There is never any doubt about the outcome; from the beginning of the story what marks Boleslo is his shrewdness, his absolute practicality of mind, while the quality that marks Judge Meeks is the wish to see the decision on the fate of a bail bond jumper, José Barreras, come out of the regular court process, the "due process of law."

Because of the Judge's dependence upon Boleslo as a bodyguard, Boleslo holds the Judge in his own hands. He is able by very slyly terrorizing Judge Meeks to produce a decision on Barreras's case which benefits everyone but the Judge, the district attorney, and the Anglo notion of due process as represented by the court. Boleslo uses the court to achieve his own ends and winds up with the self-satisfying thought that he has "interpreted" justice, or, in his words, that "real justice" has "been done in all things" (p. 8). Thus, the frontier conditions provide a man accustomed to them an opportunity to achieve his self-interest and to exercise a practical concept of "justice" based on local conditions in a time and place where the theoretically operating "court system" inherited from the East is helpless.

But there is another dimension to the story, a dimension that will offend some sensibilities. That is, Boleslo represents a large portion of the population—the Spanish Americans—out of power; and Judge Meeks, the district attorney, and the "Tejanos" who had put up the $5,000 bail bond for Barreras, represent the gringo minority who hold the land, the cash, and the chairs at government and court. This other dimension is a raw power struggle (between separate self interests with alien racial and cultural backgrounds) in which the opposing poles of interest are expressed by the Texans' blatant use in Boleslo's face of "greaser" and "Mex" and Boleslo's use, though carefully and silently to himself—because his people are out of power—of the epithet "gringo." The point is that both groups, as the story characterizes them, bitterly resent each other, and express their feelings in their terminology and in their unprincipled efforts to gain power.

The story is an interesting one, an effort to clarify in fiction the Southwest's most explosive problem. The story is perhaps the clearest statement in all of Erna's writing of these highly emotional issues. A point of criticism is that the characters, especially those of the Judge and the Texans, but also Barreras, are oversimplified. They are stereotypes which represent two sharply contrasted concepts of freedom and justice but which misrepresent

15

the real relationships between the Spanish, Mexican, and Anglo actualities of life. As Madariaga implies, the Anglo frontier was just as "free" and "unparliamentary" as the Spanish frontier, nearly as far from the seats of power in the East, and perhaps even more imaginative, even violent, in its solutions. Erna's oversimplification makes the story dated, and, no doubt to many readers, offensive. But in the light of her development as an expository writer, this story is important because it reveals Erna's experimentation early in her career with forms other than exposition to analyze and describe Southwestern culture.

In many articles Erna expresses her understanding of the Southwestern Indians. It is commonly said that no white man will ever understand "them." Probably Erna Fergusson comes closer to it than most of us do. "Senators Investigate Indians" is a striking account of a senatorial investigation of problems at the Rio Grande pueblos. Despite the tiresome hours of questioning and answering, the simple fact was that the Indians passively, but persistently, evaded the questioners. Erna selects exchanges from the testimony which amusingly illustrate the point:

[Senator to Jemez Governor]: "Did you deprive this man of water?"
[Governor]: "We did."
"Why?"
"Because he did not obey."
"What did he do?"
"He did not pay the fine."
"Why was he fined?"
"He did not obey the council."
"How did he disobey the council?"
"He did not pay the fine."
"But why did they fine him? For what?"
"He did not obey" (p. 467).

"Crusade from Santa Fe" (1936) and "Navajos: Whose Prob-

16

lem?" (1948) are Erna's two articles on the Southwestern Indian "problem" and what she thinks might be done to "solve" it. "Crusade from Santa Fe" is a brief history of the troubles on the reservations in the 1920's when New Mexico's memorable Senator Holm Bursum, a sheepman from Socorro, sponsored a bill in the United States Senate to "settle" land claims of persons not Indians within Pueblo Indian reservations. The intent of this pious deception was to validate claims to reservation lands made by outsiders—in effect, to legalize the plunder of the best of the Pueblo lands.

The Treaty of Guadalupe Hidalgo, signed by the United States Government, had guaranteed that the Pueblo Indians could retain property held under Spanish grants. According to Erna, the claims the Bursum bill sought to justify would have stripped the Pueblos of "more than ninety thousand acres of valuable lands, their principal source of income" ("Crusade from Santa Fe," p. 380). She points out that, for example, the San Juan Pueblo would have lost all but a few hundred of its four thousand acres of irrigable land. What Bursum's bill proposed, she says, was to turn all such land disputes, including disputes about water rights, over to the state courts. The bill also "provided that a survey, made to show what the adverse claims were, should serve as proof that all contested acres belonged to the white claimant, and gave the Indian no right to defend" (p. 380). The bill was defeated after the public outcry, spearheaded by a group of artists living in Santa Fe, overwhelmed the politicians.

Three important effects of this public-spirited affair, as Erna sees it, were that it organized New Mexico's artists and craftsmen for the first time into political action groups, that it gave the Indians themselves a sense that they could and would have to do something to control their own destinies, and that it led to a complete reorganization of the Indian Bureau under the imaginative John Collier, who had been a major defender of Indian rights.

17

What followed were "Day schools and better architecture. More hospitals. Encouragement of dances. . . . Action against sweat shop methods. . . . And a violent transfusion of new blood into the whole dusty bureaucracy" (pp. 386-87).

"Navajos: Whose Problem?" appeared more than a decade after "Crusade from Santa Fe." It takes up the Indian "problem" long after many of the hopeful reforms of the 1920's and the 1930's had disappeared in paperwork, after the fresh minds swept in by the Bursum affair had settled into humdrum bureaucracy or been tossed out. Curiously, the "problem" in 1947 is essentially no different. Erna sees the Indian, the Navajo, as mainly the victim of an America where the rewards and opportunities go to wealth and political power. Neither of these did the Navajo have in 1947. Though taxed for commodities, amusements, and transportation, he was, indeed, even without the power to vote. Describing the poor medical services, the low income, the eroded soil, and the bad conditions in the boarding schools, Erna points out that the Navajos have suffered most from lack of continuity in the government's programs. Long years of insensitive bureaucratic rule were followed by genuinely sensitive reform programs which "went too far" and alienated many of the Navajos themselves. When the Bureau, acting under John Collier's command, forced "3,500 head of sheep and comparable numbers of horses and cattle" to be sold or killed in a harsh effort to control erosion on the heavily over-grazed reservation, the Navajos nearly revolted. "Milder critics complain," Erna writes, "that it was badly done, at the wrong time of year, and that it removed some two thirds of the tribal wealth without proper cash compensation or provision for substitute income. Worst of all, it was done too quickly to consider the Navajo's way of thinking or to win his complete and understanding assent" ("Navajos: Whose Problem?" p. 32).

World War II followed these difficulties immediately. Again

18

the administration changed, and again the Navajos suffered from the lack of continuity. War priorities came first. As Erna writes, "One does not halt soil erosion and bring thousands of acres back into productivity, build dams to promote agriculture, nor educate a whole tribe in less than decades. It was a good long-range plan halted in mid-flight" (p. 32). Finally, Erna sees the "solution" as in the hands of the whole American people: "The transcendent need . . . is for a public opinion, informed, fair-minded, both aware and ashamed that we have allowed this crisis to arise. For we, acting through our government, have denied these people the basic rights of our civilization—education, health, a chance to make a living, and the vote" (pp. 34-35).

An equally interesting article on another historic Southwestern problem is "Tearing Down the West." Here Erna describes the erosion caused by stupid land management, or no management at all, and the Federal Government's efforts to conserve what is left. Her description of how native New Mexicans and Anglos destroyed the Rio Grande basin through years of stripping off the timber and heavy overgrazing is remarkably graphic. Erna understands clearly what is probably the greatest evil of the Southwesterner:

> This land exemplifies the propensity of man, especially white man, for destroying everything he touches . . . . In the West man has, . . . stupidly, killed the thing he needs. In fifteen years the mountain men killed off the fur-bearing animals and put themselves out of business. Hunters uselessly denuded the plains of buffalo. And all sedentary men, except the Pueblo Indians, have steadily ruined and are still ruining the country. New Mexico is not really a desert; it is a worn-out pasture (p. 332).

Never a merchant of progress, Erna could be objective about her own people's sins. Perhaps this is what her friends meant when they spoke of her "liberal spirit." Not a crusader, she was, nonetheless, often sharply critical. Taken as a whole, her articles reveal an ability to write on a wide range of Southwestern and Latin American subjects involving the people of the three cultures and the complex relationships of men to the land.

Nearly all of Erna Fergusson's books are about the Southwest or about Latin America, and they may be conveniently discussed within those two groupings. After *Dancing Gods*, she turned her attention to Latin America with *Fiesta in Mexico* (1934), *Guatemala* (1937), and *Venezuela* (1939). With *Our Southwest* (1940) she focussed again on her native country, only to turn to Hawaii in *Our Hawaii* (1942). *Chile* (1943), *Cuba* (1946), *Erna Fergusson's Albuquerque* (1947), and *Murder and Mystery in New Mexico* (1948) all followed in the 1940's. In the 1950's came the children's books, *Let's Read About Hawaiian Islands* (1950) and *Hawaii* (1950). Also published in the 1950's were *New Mexico: A Pageant of Three Peoples* (1951) and *Mexico Revisited* (1955). In the 1960's Erna published a revised edition of *New Mexico: A Pageant of Three Peoples* (1964). She had been hard at work and had nearly completed a manuscript of a book on the colorful New Mexican politician Clyde Tingley when she died on July 30, 1964. Erna's ever-popular *Mexican Cookbook* (1934), a book of New Mexican recipes, was revised in 1940 and has gone through several printings.

The first of her books on Latin America, *Fiesta in Mexico*, is really a sequel to *Dancing Gods*. It is a descriptive treatment of some of the most important Mexican-Indian festivals (*Dancing Gods* describes the Indian festivals of New Mexico and Arizona). "I have tried to see the outstanding regional and seasonal celebrations," she writes in the Introduction to *Fiesta in Mexico*, "and to understand them as fully as possible."

Typical of *Fiesta in Mexico* is chapter 2, "Fiesta Sola, Solita." Here, as elsewhere in the book, Erna describes the audience and the atmosphere as fully as she does the dancers themselves. Having suggested in the Introduction that the audience at a Mexican fiesta is as important as the dancers to the traveler who hopes to get a "varied, unforgettable, poignant picture of the people," Erna reveals the reactions of various Mexican travelers when they learn that she is headed to Tixtla to see the dances. A young señorita has been to Tixtla to pray to the Virgin but laughs at the idea that anyone would go just to see the Indians. A traveling salesman who takes frequent pulls on a bottle has often seen foreigners going to the dances but thinks it very strange. A señora on her way home to Tixtla thinks the dances pretty but regrets that the Americana will arrive too late to see the *carro*, a flower-laden parade wagon representing the birth of the Holy Virgin. The *ayudante*, Rafaelito, appalled that an American lady should go alone to the fiesta, offers to escort her.

In Tixtla, there are the booths with handmade tablecloths and napkins, sweet limes, ices, roast pork, and barbecued goat. The little boys shout to each other, "Gringa! Rafaelito's got a gringa!" At the church a thin woman clutches a baby and a small child, buying candles and making her way up the wet path on her knees. "Bells were ringing," Erna writes. "It was the hour of the Rosary, and of the rain. Penitents accepted the shower as a part of the penance and splashed along in the puddles." On the porch of the curate's house, a "brisk man" selling holy things was very polite: "Alone? You came alone? But how sad! Sit here, do me the favor" (*Fiesta in Mexico*, pp. 34-35).

The next day were the dances, a series of six or seven, each by different dancers, beginning at a different place as the preceding dance ended. There are the costumes, the dance figures, and the symbolism of the dance. Graphically she describes the dance, "Los Vaqueros": "They were a vigorous gang, and well turned-out in big hats, neckerchiefs, whips, guns, fiercely mustached masks, chaps, and spurs clanking, usually, against bare heels. They danced in a circle: a hard, stiff, masculine dance with long pauses for speeches" (p. 43).

The book is a series of vignettes of the dancers and the people of Mexican villages. There are Xochimilco Indians placing fresh flowers on an altar. They bear the flowers to the church. The long-stemmed tuberoses, the chrysanthemums, and the carnations are all white and all in tall, white vases. There are baskets of baby's breath.

> In the church they all knelt, respectful, but critical and watchful of the boys who climbed about over the altar placing the baskets and vases .... they transformed that altar into a tower of flowery white, with the cloudy baskets near the top and tall stately sheaves of tuberoses and chrysanthemums on the floor (p. 65).

While keeping her attention on the people and the culture, Erna manages unobtrusive personal observations. She senses since the Revolution, for instance, a change in many ways ugly:

> ... for the new is marked by all the corruption, inefficiency, stupidities, and abuses inevitable in a people unused to power for four hundred years. The mass still seem to cling to the earth, as though the call to power were more than they could bear. It is as though a vigorous, half-awakened race were rising in anguish from the very ground. They sit, eat, sleep, make love, work, trade, worship, live—all flat on the ground. The Indian forms a brown mysterious dado along all the stately buildings which the Spaniards raised, as though the weight of his own ignorance were still too heavy to allow him to rise (p. 89).

Fiesta in Mexico, then, is not a mere listing of all the things one ought to see while in Mexico told in language the comfortably conservative traveler from the United States might expect.

It proves Erna's ability to avoid the professional manner of the tour guide and to see and write freshly and honestly.

In *Guatemala* she widens her coverage to include history and political commentary. Still, she approaches the new subject with the sympathy and curiosity she had revealed in *Fiesta in Mexico*. She states her question clearly in the early pages. "What would Guatemala be like," she asks herself, "especially after a couple of years in Mexico . . . ?" "It is," a student had told her, "Mexico before the Revolution, still a dictatorship, still sharply divided into classes . . . . You should know it to understand Mexico better" (*Guatemala*, p. 3). *Guatemala* is a comprehensive history of the country, from the Spanish Colonial period to the period of the railroads and the United Fruit Company. There are sections on the white imperialistic mind, banana culture and business, merchants who hold the Indian in submission by keeping him in debt; and there are descriptions of the Indian consciousness, its viewpoints, and the way it works.

As in much of her other writing, Erna is most compelling in describing the Indian. She assumes that the white man does not understand the Indian, or understands him only insofar as he can force him into "useful" labor. The white businessmen and their families are just as restricted as the native population, "in spite of their screened club houses, tennis courts, and golf links. They might as well be living on an island . . . . white men repulse the human life around them . . . . a conception of him [the native worker] as a man with rights, and all that, is so remote as to seem ludicrous . . . . The banana-worker is a hand, good or bad, worth enough care to get his maximum of work, but impersonal, distant, uninteresting" (pp. 181-82). As for the natives themselves, Erna had watched them load tons of green bananas at Puerto Barrios, heavily muscled, half-naked men "with empty, dull, or smiling faces, chanting to help the rhythmic heave, or jabbering that almost inhuman singsong of the Carib speech. Democracy must come, I thought, but it will take those men a long time to know it" (p. 193).

She tells a story in *Guatemala* that has no doubt occurred in thousands of instances. An Indian boy is taken at twelve years of age against his father's debt. He is given a blanket and a machete. He gets a regular ration of beans and corn and charges all his things at the company store. He works for a year from morning till night, then asks his reckoning. He is more deeply in debt. He works another year. Older now, he buys more liquor and gifts of colored combs and glass beads for the girls he likes; for himself, a hat, a petate, calico shirts. He asks again for his account; it has more than doubled. "Hundreds of quetzales of debt," the author writes, "were his only gain for years of work from sunrise to sunset. The story has no variations. It went on so for years: man working, debt piling, life passing in flashes of joy and passion, of drunkenness and religious fervor" (p. 278). *Guatemala* foretells the revolutions of the present in Latin America.

Erna's methods are, as elsewhere, those of the honest, hardworking journalist. She has read widely before beginning her trip, but basically her material is what she sees and hears. She repeats interviews, and when two interviews contain opposing points of view or when the official view is inconsistent with what she herself sees in the streets, she points out the discrepancies. In this way she gets under the surfaces, beneath the official doctrine. The result is one of her most factual and compassionate stories. She clearly knows from firsthand observation of the exploitation of men in Latin America, and in *Guatemala* she describes it forthrightly.

Venezuela and *Chile* are weaker books than *Guatemala*, but essentially they follow its basic pattern. They are political, social, and cultural studies. But a sense of hurry pervades them which, fortunately, *Guatemala*, *Dancing Gods*, and *Fiesta in Mexico* lack. The illusion of leisurely pace of these earlier books is created

24

by Erna's sympathetically submerging her temperament in her human materials. Perhaps it was the tensions of a world soon to be at war which caused the annoyance Erna reveals in *Venezuela* and *Chile*. She makes a point of showing her personal dislike of the German militarism she sees in Latin America (although she admires the work habits of the prosperous German businessmen). When a German bus driver stops along the road to talk with another German and the two snap off the conversation with clicking heels and Heil Hitlers, Erna expresses her dislike of German authoritarianism and the democratic "inferiority" of men raised in such a culture. There are instances in both books where she fumes at the poor maid service and the uncomfortable hotel accommodations. She reveals, perhaps unconsciously, an increasing fussiness about dirt and dirty people and about the cheapening of native costumes and customs by commercialization. The Britisher with whom she takes a long drive (in *Venezuela*) is the epitome of these increasing irritations. He is upset with the country; he is afraid of the people. All his talk is about the disadvantages and dangers of having to live in South America. Unfortunately for her book, Erna identifies too closely with him. He is exaggerated. It is as if he were Erna's means of expressing her own frustrations with the country.

Another weakness in *Venezuela* and *Chile* is her casual attitude toward sections of the countries she is writing about. The early pages of *Chile*, covering the southernmost tip to the center of the country, read almost like a travel brochure. This dissatisfying effect is the result of Erna's having "seen" most of the southern section only from an airplane, her heavy reliance upon other written accounts, her decision not to go to certain important lakes because of the bad weather, and her expression of personal irritation at the weather and the people. "We saw all this in Temuco," she writes, "as we made dashes from the frigid hotel through the flooded streets to shops where leather goods and woodwork, blankets, and rough but interesting silver jewelry made us calculate not only spending-money but packing-space. Between purchases we called at a Baptist mission, a Capuchin mission, took tea or cocktails, or just gave up and went to bed in an effort to fend off that insistent cold" (pp. 80-81).

Her chapter in *Chile* on the area around Concepcion and Santiago reads as if it were taken from the World Almanac. Entitled "The Center," it gives a thumbnail history of the area and facts regarding the lottery, the opportunities, the lack of capital, and the natural resources. What she calls "classical Chile," Santiago and its surroundings, she describes mainly in quotations from other writers—Picon-Salas, Edwards, Cabero.

On the other hand, there is much good writing in these two books. One hundred pages into *Chile* Erna begins to achieve again that illusion of leisureliness by submerging herself in the consciousness of the host, the guide, or the native people, and in the geography. Her renewed interest hides the personal discomforts. She shows a clear understanding of the native's hostility toward the outsider: "There is something impudent about bouncing into a country, uninvited, to write about it" (p. 136); and her chapters on "Life in Providencia," "Rodeo at Curacaví," "La Cueva," and "Inquilino Family" are among her most perceptive. In the latter chapter she describes the bad living conditions of a tenant farmer's family and the tenant's justifiable complaints about the government and the distant landlord.

Venezuela also has some excellent passages. Erna's description of the wealthy descendants of Spanish Colonial families is acute:

They follow still the old Creole custom of going abroad to school, of living widely. They are really more at home in Paris, London, or New York than in Caracas. Of Venezuela they know nothing. The best of them withdrew during the Gómez days and took no part in politics or the social life

26

of the capital even if they stayed in Venezuela. They love Venezuela, but with a nostalgic yearning for something that never was, that can probably never be. They are as unaware of the actual conditions of that tragic country as they are of the littered, tobacco-stained streets of the capital which they are driven through in closed cars. They have lived so long under dictatorship, which repaid interference with torture, that they have lost all real sense of citizenship. The towniness that makes a man feel responsible for his place and willing to do his part about it has never developed in Venezuela (p. 71).

Our Hawaii appeared between *Our Southwest* and *Chile*. In it Erna relies more heavily upon personal observation and interview than she did in writing *Chile*. Like *Fiesta in Mexico* and *Guatemala, Our Hawaii* is the work of an active journalist, though noticeably less perceptive. It is a pleasant introduction to the pre-World War II features of the islands. But it has two serious faults. Erna fails to get below the surfaces of the romantic, glowing life of a land commercialized for the tourists. The result is that while her book never seems consciously written to stimulate tourism, it would surely have had that effect. In the South American countries she had purposely seen the squalid living conditions and had gone into the remote places. But if in Hawaii she met the economically deprived, if she saw there the frustrations of classes, of racial groups, or natives against missionaries and plantation owners, there is little suggestion of it. The chapter "Missionary Mother" tells of the courage of the wives of Protestant missionaries while barely suggesting the suffering the missionaries caused the natives. Another describes the resourcefulness of the "sugar missionary" (the plantation owner whose grandfather came as a missionary), without mentioning the feelings of the landless natives who do the sweaty work. Erna does mention the abuses of labor. There is a brief talk with an old man on a bus: "Well," he says, "they useta come round tellin' us how to vote, and we so dumb we did it. Now they come swellin' roun tellin' us same way, and we don' do it" (*Our Hawaii*, p. 183). The chapter "Malia Does What's Right" describes the moral and psychological problems of a native servant with an illegitimate son. But beyond these undeveloped instances, there is little revelation of social abuses or little discussion of the social and economic structure in Hawaii. *Our Hawaii* is Erna's least realistic book.

The other major fault, which adds to the air of unreality, is that although *Our Hawaii* was published in 1942, following the attack on Pearl Harbor, there is no mention of the war in the book. Two chapters deal specifically with the military forces on the Islands. They describe a chocolate-soldier, tinsel-navy establishment which, unfortunately, seems to have impressed Erna. She writes: "Howitzers too; and 'none better,' the Sergeant crowed. 'One of those can shoot over those mountains like nothing at all, and seven or eight miles out to sea. If anybody tried to get funny that'd be the aloha he'd get' " (p. 290). The naval officers receive leis and attend dinner parties, wives gossip about the wives of junior officers, sailors endlessly set up and knock down mock enemies in mock sea battles. Erna and the publisher should have scrapped these chapters on December 8. She later observed to friends that she had "missed the mark." Her remarks on the military seem quaint now, but they must have seemed worse than quaint to an American reader in 1942.

Cuba appeared after Erna Fergusson had served her wartime government in Washington with the Division of Education. She had worked in the Office of the Coordinator of Inter-American affairs where, according to her friend Dorothy Woodward, she had entertained wives of visiting Latin American dignitaries. Tiring of official work, she quit her job and went off to study Cuba. The book which resulted is a good one-volume history. The reader is introduced to charming ladies and gentlemen full of stories about Cuba's past glories and terrors and her present achievements. Although Erna paints a compelling picture of the richly varied beauty of the Cuban landscape, she fails, as in *Our Hawaii*, to search out the island's poor.

Her chapter "The Colonial Complex" opens this vigorously written essay on Cuba's history from the earliest explorations to the 1940's. The closing chapter, "Two Cubas," is a comprehensive essay on Cuban music, drama, fiction, poetry, and painting. Erna's materials are drawn from a wide variety of writers on Cuba—ranging from Cuban historians hypercritical of U.S. interference to conservative American rationalizers of intervention—but she avoids inserting long quotations, a serious fault of the first one hundred pages of *Chile*. What she does is to digest the scholarly books, then write concise essays using their information and views. The result is a very readable text containing a variety of viewpoints. Throughout the book she maintains a strict objectivity, refusing either to rationalize or to deny U.S. excesses; and she recommends that a book by Portell-Vila, a critical attack upon the U.S., be required reading for all students of Latin America. Her objectivity is admirable, especially when one considers that the book was written during wartime.

To read *Cuba* is to sympathize with the people's painful struggle for freedom from foreign domination, both Spanish and American. And it is to understand that American intervention, even in those cases where it was not entirely motivated by selfishness, created an increasing hostility toward the United States in the minds of the Cuban people. For introducing the general reader to the causes of Cuba's break with America, there is perhaps no better one-volume study.

The last of Erna's books on Latin America is *Mexico Revisited*. It is a different kind of book from *Cuba*, much more the traveler's overview of that vast and complex country, much less a key to un-derstanding the people and their problems. *Mexico Revisited* lacks the in-depth studies of Mexican-Spanish and Mexican-American relations as well as the ideas and historical and scholarly theses of *Cuba*. It is fast-moving and far-reaching in terms of geography and population, but it lacks intimate visits with natives. The book is structured around an auto tour of Mexico with side trips by bus and taxi. It is a form which worked well for a small coun-try like Cuba, but which breaks down on so immense a country as Mexico. Still, *Mexico Revisited* is a good outline of the people and colorful places of Mexico. Yet it is only an outline, not a thorough study.

Erna Fergusson's first book on the Southwest was *Dancing Gods*. It is structured much like *Fiesta in Mexico*—emphasizing dances and their meanings—and serves neatly as a companion to that vol-ume. A short Foreword plainly states Erna's attitude toward the Indian, an attitude she maintains throughout her life. "South-western Indians," she writes, "have no better friends than artists, who recognize that the Indian is essentially an artist. They value his art in all its forms, they help him without condescension, and they respect his integrity too much to try to make him over into something foreign" (*Dancing Gods*, p. v).

She is completely in sympathy with the Indian and his threat-ened way of life, and she occasionally seems to practice an inverse discrimination against the Anglo intruders. She is down on Indian agents and the efforts of government bureaus to educate the Indian for assimilation. A typical passage from *Dancing Gods* reads: "The avowed purpose is to prepare the young Indian for citizenship and for making a living. Actually very little attention is paid to his spe-cial needs or aptitudes or to the revival or maintenance of his arts and crafts. The result is to unfit him for life among his own peo-ple" (p. 25). She sees the influence on the dance of easily

30

purchased American commercial goods as inevitably degrading, and her attitude toward tourists is condescending. The condescension is undoubtedly a carryover of what she had sometimes felt while she herself was a tour guide. She speaks of tour guides "who fight a hopeless fight against dust and heat and glare and tepid drinking-water to make comfortable people who cannot be made comfortable short of real comfort" (p. 162).

Most of *Dancing Gods* is made up of descriptions of dance ceremonies Erna had often watched. Each chapter describes the process of the ceremony as it unfolds. Besides detailing the action of the dances, Erna comments upon their meaning. She notes about the corn dance, for example, that the Koshare, early in the dance, rehearse the history of the tribe in pantomime. There is the going out and coming in of the runners to announce the approach of enemies—Navajo, Comanche, Apache—the forming of lines to protect the pueblo and the crops from the raiders, and the calling of the participants to dance for the gods to protect and mature the crops. Recently I went to Santo Domingo to the corn dance. I noticed many of the details Erna mentions: the difference between the dance steps of the men and women, the sun-yellow color of the top feathers of the banner, the sudden changes of rhythm and step in the dance, the dry corn husk topknots of the Koshare, and the way the Koshare act as valets to the dancers, stepping in to retie loosened sashes, rattles, or feathers while the dance goes on.

Essentially, Erna Fergusson respects the Indian's secrets and his dignity. She understands the distance the Indian must keep between himself and the white man: "They come out of their world sometimes to speak to us, for they understand our language; but when they withdraw into their world, we cannot follow" (*Dancing Gods*, p. 276). It is Erna's dignified handling of these colorful but mysterious ceremonies that makes the reader feel he has sat respectfully beside the Indian. *Dancing Gods* remains a lasting contribu-

31

tion, an excellent introduction to the Southwestern Indian and his ritualistic life.

After *Dancing Gods*, Erna waited until 1940 to publish her next book on the Southwest, *Our Southwest*. It is one of her least satisfying books because, as in *Mexico Revisited*, she attempts to cover too large a geographical and cultural area, although her observations and her pattern for touring the Southwest are interesting in themselves. She sees the Southwest as neatly divided into "winter and summer country." "The desert and near-desert country from San Antonio, Texas, to Los Angeles, California," she observes, "is delightful in winter; much of it is too hot for vacationing in summer. The northern half of New Mexico and Arizona and certain southward-reaching spurs of the Rockies are lofty enough to offer a fine summer climate; much of it is cold in winter" (p. 20). After an introductory chapter, "What Is the Southwest?," she opens with Fort Worth and the cattle business (Fort Worth is the easternmost point of "her" Southwest), then moves across Texas, through El Paso into Arizona, and briefly into southern Colorado. Finally, she takes us back into New Mexico's Rio Grande Valley and eastward to the high plains and the Texas Panhandle.

Our Southwest is packed with sound information, interesting interpretations, but not always applicable generalizations about the nature of Southwesterners. The introductory essay suggests that the character of Southwestern life and thought has been most marked by the aridity which forced settlers from the well-watered East to find altogether new means of making a living. The result, as Erna sees it, was that only the lucky stayed on. Those with a practical plan who tried, for instance, to make over a quarter section of New Mexican prairie into an Illinois corn field were inevitably beaten by the sun and the hot, drying winds. Success was a matter of caprice, not of "steady thrift and the homely virtues" (p. 17). The settler struck gold or oil, hit an artesian well that turned his

32

desert patch into an oasis, or happened to have homesteaded in the right place when the railroad came through and turned his pasture into building sites. The strong man, facing an indomitable land, simply moved on in search of "dependability," of something he could make over more successfully. "I know more Albuquerque people in California now," Erna says, "than in Albuquerque" (p. 18).

The other shaping forces of the Southwestern character as Erna sees it are the ancient Indian cultures and the modern pueblos, the Spanish and Mexican presence, the sense of cooperation or "democratic friendliness" caused by the difficulty of surviving on the frontier, and the necessity for exaggeration as a means of making fun. Facing this "hell of a country," the settler "in his irritation secreted a kind of humor" which depended upon exaggeration (p. 16). She mentions the Texan, the man who "was for law if he made it, for order if he enforced it," and who "felt no compunction about changing a law which no longer fitted the case" (p. 28).

Erna Fergusson, as always, is sympathetic to the Indian and the Spanish American, both of whom she recognizes as long-exploited, but not "exploitable" much longer. She finds the civilization of the Rio Grande Valley of a high kind—based on graciousness and a toleration of varied opinions and religions. The book has an informative chapter on the tuberculosis cure as an Albuquerque industry, another on the history of the Fred Harvey restaurants, one on the Navajo, one on Taos, and one on the economic and social problems of the northern New Mexican villages. Then, moving eastward again, her book follows the high, summer country to the Panhandle.

Erna Fergusson's *Albuquerque* was followed by *Murder and Mystery in New Mexico* in 1948. The first is a patchwork of observations on New Mexico's largest city; much of the material had appeared earlier in Erna's articles in the *Century Magazine* and

33

in the Albuquerque newspapers. The style is much the same as that of the material she was writing in the 1920's for the hometown readers, and the book, as a whole, is of little concern to any but Albuquerquians and students of Erna Fergusson. The second is a more interesting book, although it fails to accomplish what the Introduction suggests it will. It is a collection of murder cases from New Mexico's past, some of them unsolved, others officially solved but still open to much speculation. In her Introduction Erna raises interesting questions, but, in failing to develop answers to them, she misses an excellent opportunity to analyze "violence" in the Southwest. What caused the murder? Was no one else partly or entirely to blame? Why was no one else brought to trial? "Probably," she theorizes in the Introduction, "people are never so much themselves as when they are killing or being killed. Perhaps there is no better way to know a people than to understand why they kill." Sometimes, she continues, killing is thought of as a "manly and needful act," sometimes "an intolerable offense" (*Murder and Mystery in New Mexico*, p. 13). Sometimes the evil of men not killers themselves forces other men to become killers.

Erna's last book on the Southwest, *New Mexico: A Pageant of Three Peoples*, stands with *Dancing Gods, Fiesta in Mexico, Guatemala,* and *Cuba* as one of her best. It represents the culmination of a lifetime of living in, traveling about, and studying her home state with an affectionate but often critical mind. It is a serious effort to explain the past and bring the explanation to bear on the realities of the present. What Erna ultimately has in mind is stated in the Foreword: "The rites of prehistoric Indians and of Europeans of the Middle Ages are still practiced here. The two frontiers—Spanish and United States—met and fused in New Mexico .... It is of greater value, now that our country has been forced into world leadership, that in New Mexico the peoples of three cultures have successfully worked out a life together" (p. vii).

The book is divided into three major sections, entitled "Indian," "Spanish," and "Gringo." The sections contain chapters on the history and present conditions of each culture considered both separately and in relation to the other. Pairs of chapters in Part I suggest the subject matter: "The Traditional Navajo," "The Modern Navajo"; and "The Warlike Apache," "The Modern Apache." Part II, "Spanish," links such chapters as "Spanish Colonial Life," "Our Spanish Heritage," and "The New New Mexican." Part III, "Gringo," contains chapters on "The Federal Man," "Water," and on New Mexico's artists—painters, novelists, and photographers.

As in much of her earlier writing on the Indian, Erna shows an understanding of the difficulties he has in adapting his ancient faith to the modern world. She appreciates his efforts, and she clearly is offering his struggles as a model for Anglos who have lost their own faith in a world increasingly materialistic and warlike. "To this mid-twentieth century the Pueblo brings old beliefs that may light his life with beauty or shadow it with fear," she writes, "but that surely pervade his daily thinking. . . . The dance that may impress the white onlooker as a triumph of art in step, costume, music, and choreography is to the Indian . . . the renewal of an ancient faith and the bulwark of his security" (*New Mexico: A Pageant of Three Peoples*, p. 52).

In the same way, she offers the moral ideal of the Pueblo as an example. The fundamental social conception in Pueblo life and thought is the good of the group. Hence, morality is the act of conforming to custom and authority and the skill or correctness with which one conforms. To neglect custom and authority is to bring evil upon the community: "The idea of individual sin or reward for individual good does not enter into Pueblo thought. A man's worth is computed not by what he has amassed for himself, but by what good he has done his group" (p. 38). She is not so naive as to think everyone can live like the Indians, but she is clearly hoping that by defining their way of life she can stimulate a new appreciation for the value of the Indian culture, and, perhaps, for lasting values in the Southwest's whole cultural heritage.

Of the Spanish heritage, Erna displays an equal appreciation. She shows how it daily affects the art, architecture, and language of the modern Southwest. Her emphasis, as with the Indian, is on the value of that heritage for the present rather than on the irrecoverable past. If she is not herself a historian's historian, she is in this book everything she had tried to be: one who could make the past relevant to the modern man of affairs, the non-scholar, and the working man.

Throughout the book, she is critical of the Anglo interloper— the preacher who condemns those not of his specific faith, the developer who plans a scenic highway across the last mountain retreat or who greedily sees a reservoir in every ancient gorge. What Erna Fergusson wants is that progress and profit be kept in balance with the Southwest's uniquely beautiful and profoundly religious geographical and cultural heritage. She clearly suggests that unless the two are balanced, the Southwestern heritage will live only as a commercial resource and not as a means of clarifying life.

Erna Fergusson is a difficult writer to place. Her work is not a part of a literary tradition, but essentially an isolated phenomenon in the Southwest (she wrote fifty years later than the first great popularizer, Charles F. Lummis, and her work is very different from that of Mary Austin and Paul Horgan). She wrote little fiction and no poetry. Hence, she cannot be treated with the usual devices of literary criticism. The difficulty of writing about her is compounded by the fact that her own life clearly was a part of a rich cultural tradition and was overshadowed by the lives of her more colorful father and grandfather, to say nothing of the work of her brothers, Francis Fergusson the drama critic and Harvey Fergusson the novelist. It is nearly impossible to view her apart from these brilliant figures. She is inseparably a Fergusson and a Huning and, therefore, a chartered Southwesterner.

Yet Erna was, apart from her writing, an unusual person, a genuine force for humanity in the Southwest. Persons who knew her well say that the best of Erna Fergusson was the woman, the human being, and that her profoundest qualities came through more clearly in her character than in her writing. She was an intensely loyal friend who was accustomed to put down gossip with "Why do you talk that way? You don't know that is so!" She cared nothing for the disapproval of the social highbrows and once shocked the dignified at an important university affair by riding to campus in a pickup truck. She had a sparkling sense of humor, but she was a scrapper when she sensed that one of her many friends needed protection. Once, when a visitor proposed to make use of the cheap labor on an Indian reservation, she rose in a roomful of people with the stern warning, "You try that, and I'll fight you!" Of her personal life she never complained. As one friend put it, "She embraced life." She never spoke of the increasing illness of her last years, and she looked for the facts as well as for the best qualities in other people. As an old lady she took on a countless variety of visitors at her home in Albuquerque, always in sight of the Sandia Mountains and the cottonwood trees, and, with daring, she continued to make long trips to gather material for books, often driving alone, well into her last years.

In a day before jet aircraft, fast cars, super highways, and air-conditioned motels, and in a time when the American Southwest and Latin America were still remote and exotic places on the map, seldom visited by any but wealthy, retired people with whole winters and summers of leisure time, Erna Fergusson helped make the Southwest and Latin America seem like real and accessible places for the general American reader. She was read widely. Features on her Koshare Tours and reviews of her books appeared in nearly every newspaper in the country. She was the twentieth century's popularizer of the Southwest and a spokesman for those little-understood people, Indians and Spanish Americans. Her writing made Americans less provincial at a time when the United States was being forced out of isolation into world domination. There is no doubt that Erna Fergusson helped to ease the distress of this transition by preparing the way to understanding in the minds of the American people.

It is to her credit that in this powerful position of influence, she was a responsible student and journalist. Although in many details her accounts suffer from the evanescence to which all journalism is a victim, her spirit, her sympathy, and her understanding of the psychological and economic problems of minorities facing an overwhelming and alien civilization are relevant today. In her best books she is a careful craftsman, and throughout her work runs that capacity for enlightened criticism necessary to the journalist who seeks to interpret his own broad cultural backgrounds to a mass audience.

Selected Bibliography

BOOKS BY ERNA FERGUSSON

SOUTHWEST

Dancing Gods: Indian Ceremonials of New Mexico and Arizona (New York: Alfred A. Knopf, 1931).

Erna Fergusson's Albuquerque (Albuquerque: Merle Armitage Editions, 1947).

Mexican Cookbook (Santa Fe: The Rydal Press, 1934; revised edition, 1940; sixth printing, reillustrated, Albuquerque: University of New Mexico Press, 1945).

Murder and Mystery in New Mexico (Albuquerque: Merle Armitage Editions, 1948).

New Mexico: A Pageant of Three Peoples (New York: Alfred A. Knopf, 1951; second edition, revised, 1964).

Our Southwest (New York: Alfred A. Knopf, 1940).

FOREIGN TRAVEL

Chile (New York: Alfred A. Knopf, 1943).

Cuba (New York: Alfred A. Knopf, 1946).

Fiesta in Mexico (New York: Alfred A. Knopf, 1934).

Guatemala (New York: Alfred A. Knopf, 1937).

Mexico Revisited (New York: Alfred A. Knopf, 1955).

Our Hawaii (New York: Alfred A. Knopf, 1942).

Venezuela (New York: Alfred A. Knopf, 1939).

CHILDREN'S BOOKS

Hawaii (Grand Rapids, Michigan: The Fideler Company, 1950).

Let's Read About Hawaiian Islands (Grand Rapids, Michigan: The Fideler Company, 1950).

ARTICLES BY ERNA FERGUSSON

"Acoma, the City of the Sky," *New Mexico Highway Journal*, I (October, 1923), 4-5.

"Adobe or Not Adobe," *Country Life*, LIX (January, 1931), 65-66.

"Americanism, My Definition—A Symposium," *New Mexico Quarterly*, VI (November, 1936), 295.

"Ceremonial Dances of the Pueblos," *Travel*, LVIII (December, 1931), 15-19.

"The Coronado Cuarto Centennial," *New Mexico Quarterly*, X (May, 1940), 67-71.

"Crusade From Santa Fe," *North American Review*, CCXLII (December, 1936), 376-87.

"Festival in Chalma," *The Inter-American*, III (August, 1944), 16-19.

"From Redskins to Railroads," *Century Magazine*, CXIII (November, 1926), 23-31.

"From Rodeo to Rotary," *Century Magazine*, CXIII (December, 1926), 199-207.

"Gabriela Mistral," *The Inter-American Monthly*, I (August, 1942), 26-27.

"Guatemala Is Swept and Garnished," *Country Life*, LXXI (November, 1936), 40-41, 105-06.

"Guatemalan Journey," *House and Garden*, XCII (November, 1947), 198-201.

"Indians of Mexico and New Mexico," *New Mexico Quarterly*, IV (August, 1934), 169-73.

"John Collier in New Mexico," *New Mexico Quarterly*, VI (August, 1936), 225-26.

"Justice As Interpreted," *New Mexico Quarterly*, III (February, 1933), 3-8 (story).

"Laughing Priests," *Theatre Arts Monthly*, XVII (August, 1933), 657-62.

"The Merry Festival of the Dead," *Travel*, LXIII (June, 1934), 8-14, 53-54.

"Modern Apaches of New Mexico," *The American Indian*, VI (Summer, 1951), 3-14.

"Navajos: Whose Problem?" *New Mexico Quarterly*, XVIII (Spring, 1948), 25-35.

"New Mexico—State of Many Ages," *Think*, XVI (August, 1950), 7-9, 24.

"New Mexico's Mexicans," *Century Magazine*, CXVI (August, 1928), 437-44.

"The New New Mexican," *New Mexico Quarterly*, XIX (Winter, 1949), 417-26.

"Perpetual Pagans," *Scribner's Magazine*, XCII (November, 1932), 293-95.

"The Sad Feast of Oaxaca," *American Mercury*, XXXI (January, 1934), 8-15.

"Senators Investigate Indians," *American Mercury*, XXIII (August, 1931), 464-68.

"Tearing Down the West," *Yale Review*, XXV (December, 1935), 331-43.
"What of Our Indian G.I.?" *Americas*, II (July, 1950), 17-21, 46.
"A Writer's View of Southwest Libraries," *Libraries in the Southwest: Their Growth, Strength, Needs* (Los Angeles: University of California Library, 1955), 3-11.
"You Yanquis," *New Mexico Quarterly*, XII (August, 1942), 261-71.

MISCELLANEOUS SHORT WORKS BY ERNA FERGUSSON

NOTE: Erna Fergusson wrote a number of articles for the long-defunct Albuquerque *Herald* in the 1920's. The only known copies of that newspaper are in the office of the County Clerk of Bernalillo County, New Mexico. An uncertain number of the "Do You Remember?" articles appeared in the *Herald* in 1922 and 1923. The Albuquerque Public Library has typed copies of many of the "Do You Remember?" articles. Listed here are those articles cited in the text.

"Do You Remember the First Street Car?" Albuquerque *Herald*, XIII (February 12, 1923), p. 2.
"Do You Remember the First Train?" Albuquerque *Herald*, XIII (January 15, 1923), p. 8.
"Do You Remember Freighting Across the Plains?" Albuquerque *Herald*, XIII (January 22, 1923), p. 3.

NOTE: Erna Fergusson wrote a great many book reviews, some of which may be found in her scrapbooks in the Erna Fergusson Collection, Coronado Room, University of New Mexico Library. She also lectured widely. Notes for some of the lectures are also to be found in the Coronado Room at the University of New Mexico Library. I give here a sampling of her lectures in chronological order to reveal her range over a period of less than ten years.

"Chile in Transition," Conference of Latin America in Social and Economic Transition, University of New Mexico, Albuquerque (April 14-15, 1943).
"Mexico in the Modern World," Inter-American Workshop, University of Wyoming, Laramie (July 8, 1943).
"Indians and Ladinos in Guatemala," Meeting of Society of Women Geographers, Washington, D. C. (November 25, 1944).

41

"International Relations with Latin America," Meeting of Educators Interested in International Relations, Albuquerque (May 17, 1945).

"Who Really Carried the Message to Garcia?" Gallup Rotary Club, Gallup, N. M. (October 9, 1946).

"The Individual's Role in the Pan-American Problem," University of Texas, Pan-American Day (April 14, 1947).

"Malinche," Scripps College, Claremont, California (March 16, 1948).

"The Americas Must Serve Mankind," New Mexico Military Institute, Pan-American Day, Roswell (April 14, 1948).

"Why New Mexico?" Farmington Business and Professional Women's Club, Farmington, N. M. (April 29, 1949).

"The Navajo Situation," Friday Morning Club, Los Angeles, California (1949).

"Our Old Spanish Customs," Las Cruces Writers Club, Las Cruces, N. M. (April 18, 1950).

WORKS ABOUT ERNA FERGUSSON

Cassidy, Louise Lowber, "A 'Delight Maker,' " Sunset Magazine, LIV (January, 1925), 38-39.

Eason, Helga H., "Erna Fergusson," Wilson Library Bulletin, XXIX (June, 1955), 748.

"Editorial Notes," American Mercury, XXIII (August, 1931), xx.

Fergusson, Harvey, Home in the West: An Inquiry into My Origins (New York: Duell, Sloan and Pearce, 1945).

Fisher, Irene, "Erna Fergusson," Albuquerque Review (February 8, 1962), 2.

Keleher, William A., "Erna Fergusson," The Historical Society of New Mexico Hall of Fame Essays (Albuquerque, 1965), 27-54.

McMullen, Frances Drewry, "Ask Miss Fergusson," Woman Citizen, XI (January, 1927), 26-27, 41-42.

Powell, Lawrence Clark, "First Lady of Letters," New Mexico Magazine, XL (March, 1962), 22-23, 37-39.

Woodward, Dorothy, "Erna Fergusson," New Mexico Quarterly, XXII (Spring, 1952), 75-89.

42

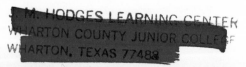